My VISIT TO The EMPIRE STATE BUILDING

and New York City

EMPIRE STATE
BUILDING

Sold exclusively at the Empire State Building

© 2010 Designed and Published by Terrell Creative
P.O. Box 34260
Kansas City, MO 64120

ISBN-13: 978-1-56944-407-8

Select photos by Joe Luman © Terrell Creative,
Page 4, Photo by Lewis Hine, *The Empire State Building Under Construction*, Circa 1930,
Museum of the City of New York (L.638.8) and skyline photo courtesy Library of Congress
Page 7, (clockwise) Photo © Randy Harris/Dreamstime.com,
© Gary718/Dreamstime.com and © Andrew Kazmierski/Dreamstime.com,
Page 16, construction photo courtesy Library of Congress,
Page 23, (lower right corner) photo courtesy Augustus Sherman Collection/National Park Service
and Page 27, (lower left and middle) from Wikipedia photos © Urban and © David Corby

So my dad is going to New York to photograph the Empire State Building and New York City and he is taking me along as his assistant, which is very cool. I will be missing school, (bummer right?—so totally NOT!) and my creative writing teacher has given me the task of keeping a sort of journal of my trip, with photos, postcards and souvenirs of other cool stuff I find along the way.

This has to be the greatest assignment EVER! So here goes ...

This was on our first day. We were ready to hop on the subway and check out Empire State Building!

This is me in NYC, ready to go—but come on Dad, enough with the photos already.

Here is some info I found on the history of Empire State Building:

The Empire State Building was conceived by Jakob Raskob, who created General Motors. He wanted to build the tallest building in world. So did Walter Chrysler, who started Chrysler Corporation. These two car builders were racing to build their buildings.

Chrysler finished his building first, and for a few months he owned the world's tallest building, 1,046 feet tall.

Work on the Empire State Building was started on March 17, 1930 and was finished 13 months later.

The building is 1,472 feet tall, measured to the top of the antenna. The top of the roof is measured at 1,250. The Empire State Building was the world's tallest building until the World Trade Center Towers were completed in the 1970s.

This postcard shows workers on Empire State Building. The photo was taken by Lewis Hine, who was a famous photographer.

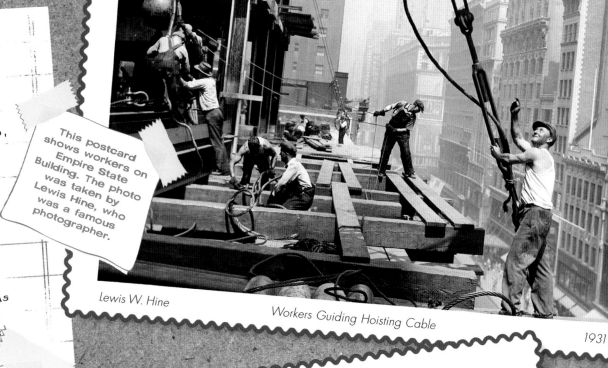

Lewis W. Hine

Workers Guiding Hoisting Cable

1931

Look at the super cool postcards I bought! This one shows the Chrysler Building & Empire State Building right after they were built.

Empire State Building

Chrysler Building

State Building
RK CITY · NYC
State Building
RK CITY · NYC
State Buildin
State Buildin
RK CITY ·
State Bu
State Bu
RK CITY
State B
RK CITY

"It was beauty killed the beast."

Empire State Building has been featured in many famous movies. Possibly the most famous movie of all featuring the Empire State Building is King Kong. I saw this cool display of all of this King Kong movie stuff.

5

KING KONG
THE EIGHTH WONDER OF THE WORLD

KING KONG
FAY WRAY and ROBERT ARMSTRONG
BRUCE CABOT
EDGAR WALLACE

The Empire State Building is known for the different colors that are used to shine on the top of the building. There are three levels of color that can be changed. The top section is the skinny part, or the mast. These colors are changed electronically. The bottom two sections are large white spotlights that have metal frames that allow building staff electricians to place colored discs over the lights to change the colors that shine on the building. It is kind of like placing colored cellophane over a flashlight, only lots bigger.

You can go to the Empire State Building website and see the schedule for the lights and what colors they will be and what the occasion is. I wonder if they would change the lights for my birthday.

Manhattan Bridge   Brooklyn Bridge

Statue of Liberty   Ellis Island

This is what the lights looked like the first night I was in New York. White, white, white - it's like their traditional colors or something for everyday stuff. Pretty cool, huh?

The first light to shine on Empire State Building was to celebrate the election of Franklin D. Roosevelt as President in 1932.

Check It Out

Look at all the different pictures I found of Empire State Building. The lights are different colors in each one!

7

Empire State Building

1,472 feet

102nd-Floor Observatory

1,250 feet

Fun Facts

1,472 feet high with 102 stories

1 year and 45 days to construct

7 million man hours of work

16,000 people work in the Empire State Building

35,000 visitors daily

I had never stopped to think about how often I have seen pictures of the Empire State Building on TV, in magazines and in movies. But since I knew I was going to get to go visit it, I see it all the time. Now that you have read this, I bet you will begin to notice it, too.

My dad came to visit New York City and the Empire State Building when he was my age, way, way, way back in 1964. Sorry dad, but you are old. His father, my grandfather, was born in New York City long before the Empire State Building was built. He was 17 when he saw it going up. It must have been exciting to see it rise so quickly!

Here I traced the Empire State Building. Wish I knew how to draw that well.

This was a neat picture that my dad took. It was a cloudy day but then suddenly the sun shined just on the Empire State Building.

These coin-operated binoculars are super cool! It was amazing how much I could see.

The wind was crazy strong at the top. Talk about your bad hair days.

The observation deck on the 86th floor is really awesome. You are so far above the ground. The wind can blow really hard up here. It was funny watching people's hair fly up on their head. One man had his hat blow right off his head and out over New York City. I lost sight of it as it headed over the East River!

It seems like more people line up for the view looking south to lower Manhattan than any other direction, although that could be due to the cold wind that was blowing from the Northwest when I was there.

There are sooooo many cool places in New York. I tried to label them on this photo we took, but there just wasn't enough room!

Manhattan Bridge

Brooklyn Bridge

EAST RIVER

VERRAZANO-NARROWS BRIDGE —THIS BRIDGE CONNECTS BROOKLYN TO STATEN ISLAND.

China Town
Little Italy

On the clearest days you can see five states from up here, including, of course, New York. The states are New Jersey and Pennsylvania that you see looking to the west, and Connecticut and Massachusetts that are to the northeast.

This photo is looking south. We used a wide angle lens to get this picture. That is photographer talk. It means you see a lot more of the city in one photo.

Metropolitan Life Building World's tallest building in 1909.

Flatiron Building

Welcome to New Jersey
Statue of Liberty
Liberty Island
Ellis Island
"Ground Zero"
Woolworth Building
Hudson River
This is the Holland Tunnel ventilation shaft —cool huh?
Greenwich Village
Did you know… There are like more than 1.6 MILLION people living in Manhattan Island???
WOW!

Statue of Liberty

WELCOME!

0104400490793

One morning we took the subway to Battery Park and from there caught the ferry to Liberty Island. Inside Battery Park is Castle Clinton, a real fort built to defend Manhattan Island during the War of 1812. While we waited in line to board the ferry, I read up on Lady Liberty. The people of France gave the statue as a gift of friendship to the people of the United States. The Statue of Liberty has been called the universal symbol of freedom and democracy. Sculptor Frédéric-Auguste Bartholdi designed the statue. It was built in France and then shipped to the United States. It was supposed to be in place in time to celebrate the 100th birthday of the United States, but it did not arrive until ten years later.

Goldman Sachs Tower
Tallest building in New Jersey
42 Floors, 781 Feet

Here is the
Empire State Building!
102 Floors, 1,472 Feet

Woolworth Building
Tallest Building in the
world from 1913 to 1930

THE
STATUE
OF
LIBERTY
NATIONAL MONUMENT
&
ELLIS
ISLAND

VALID FOR Battery Park with Monument
03/17/2009 Check In 1:00 PM
One admission
TRIP & TOURS LAST ENTRANCE
TO THE MONUMENT AT 330PM
ADULT RESERVE & Monument
Price 12.00 Order ID
VISITOR
Enjoy your visit!
Transaction#196960 Node# aguzman Approval# 017660
Transaction date 03/17/2009 Transaction time 12:44 PM

The tablet in her hand reads July 4th, 1776 in Roman numerals. The Statue of Liberty arrived in New York Harbor in June of 1885. The 350 individual pieces packed in 214 crates took four months to put back together. She was officially dedicated on Oct. 28th 1886, a centennial gift ten years later.

40 Wall Street
World's Tallest Building from
April 30 to May 27, 1930

15

The New Colossus by Emma Lazarus

Not like the brazen giant of Greek fame,

With conquering limbs astride from land to land;

Here at our sea-washed, sunset gates shall stand

A mighty woman with a torch, whose flame

Is the imprisoned lightning, and her name

Mother of Exiles. From her beacon-hand

Glows world-wide welcome; her mild eyes command

The air-bridged harbor that twin cities frame.

"Keep, ancient lands, your storied pomp!" cries she

With silent lips. "Give me your tired, your poor,

Your huddled masses yearning to breathe free,

The wretched refuse of your teeming shore.

Send these, the homeless, tempest-tost to me,

I lift my lamp beside the golden door!"

I cut this photo out of a brochure that told about
Frédéric Auguste Bartholdi, wow, what a name,
I think he was French or something. Anyway, he was a
sculptor and this is Lady Liberty being made.

The seven rays (points) of the crown represent the seven seas and the continents of the world.

Check out these interesting facts about the statue:

The copper used to cover the statue weighs 62,000 pounds.

The weight of the steel in the statue is 250,000 pounds.

The statue can sway up to three inches in winds of 50 miles per hour.

The torch can sway up to six inches.

There are 25 windows in the crown.

Inscribed on the tablet is "JULY IV MDCCLXXVI", which is July 4, 1776, the date of American Independence.

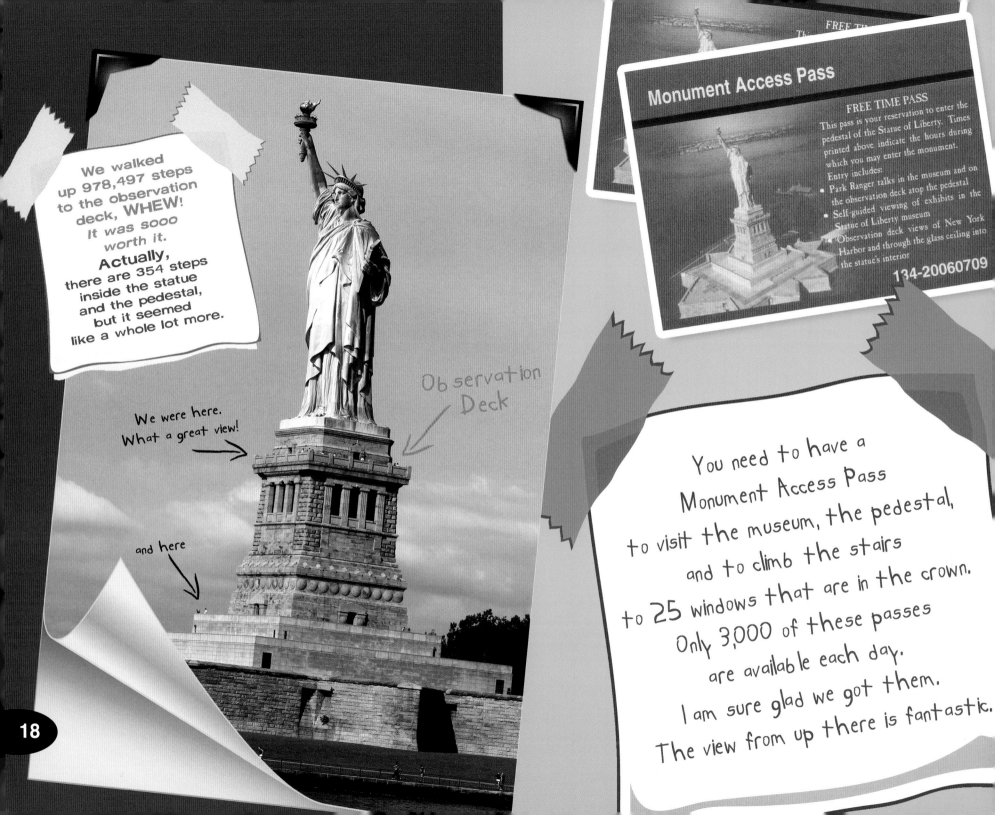

We walked up 978,497 steps to the observation deck, **WHEW!** It was sooo worth it. **Actually,** there are 354 steps inside the statue and the pedestal, but it seemed like a whole lot more.

Observation Deck

We were here. What a great view!

and here

Monument Access Pass

FREE TIME PASS
This pass is your reservation to enter the pedestal of the Statue of Liberty. Times printed above indicate the hours during which you may enter the monument.
Entry includes:
• Park Ranger talks in the museum and on the observation deck atop the pedestal
• Self-guided viewing of exhibits in the Statue of Liberty museum
• Observation deck views of New York Harbor and through the glass ceiling into the statue's interior

134-20060709

You need to have a Monument Access Pass to visit the museum, the pedestal, and to climb the stairs to 25 windows that are in the crown. Only 3,000 of these passes are available each day. I am sure glad we got them. The view from up there is fantastic.

18

The museum we walked through shows the models of different parts of the statue, this is me standing by a foot! Pretty cool, huh?

19

Ellis Island

On New Year's Day, 1892, 15-year-old Annie Moore became the first immigrant to be processed through the Ellis Island immigration station.

Ellis Island was open from 1892 all the way to 1954. That's like 62 years - WOW!

When it was open, Ellis Island processed something like over 12 million people. That's a whole bunch of steamship passengers!

This "Wall of Honor" has over 600,000 names of people that emigrated through Ellis Island. That's Manhattan that you see across the Hudson River.

My day at Ellis Island was super special for my dad and me because we searched for information on our ancestors. They immigrated from Latvia in 1899. Being at Ellis Island in the very place that my great-grandparents once were was very special!

Here are photos of my great-grandparents that we researched while at Ellis Island.

Did You Know . . . that 40 percent of America can totally trace their history through Ellis Island? How neat is that?!?

This is one of the stations where you could do a search for your family's passenger records.

This was a super cool exhibit. You look at it one way and it's the American Flag—the other way and it's a bunch of faces.

I heard that there are around 2 million people who check out Ellis Island EVERY YEAR! Just think—this year I was one of them.

Registry Room or Great Hall, pre-1916
Take a look at ALL THE PEOPLE!

This is the Great Hall—it was like the place everyone was brought when they came to Ellis Island.

Times Square is more than a square. It consists of five blocks from 42nd street to 47th street where Broadway crosses 7th Avenue.

In Manhattan, the avenues run north south and the streets run east west, but Broadway kind of runs diagonally across Manhattan in a north south direction. It is easy to go the wrong direction when you are walking until you learn this.

The Jumbotron sign above the M & M's store was really fun. The red M & M was acting like King Kong on top of the Empire State Building.

Times Square is awesome!

Where do I start? How can you explain Times Square to someone that

has never been there before? Lights, People, Taxi's, Broadway Shows,

M & M's, Hershey's, Toy Stores, High Definition billboards; you could

spend days in Times Square and never see everything there is to see.

My mom and dad took me to a Broadway play.

I was not very excited about it but I was way wrong.

Mama Mia! was sooo much fun. We had front-row seats in the

balcony. I found myself singing along with my mom and dad.

I was glad that none of my

friends could see me!

We rode the subway everywhere we went, even out to this station in Queens to get this photo of the Empire State Building in the distance.

When riding the subway you need to remember that the downtown trains take you south to lower Manhattan, and the uptown trains take you north to Midtown and beyond.

MTA MetroCard

Insert this way / This

The New York Stock Exchange is like the largest in the world! How cool is that?

WALL ST
←9-15
EXCHANG

DID YOU KNOW ...
there are
383 Wall Streets
in the world?
WOW!

It was a short walk from Wall Street to Ground Zero where the World Trade Center Twin Towers once stood.

When the first tower was completed in 1972, it officially was to tallest building in the world until 1974 when the Sears Tower in Chicago was completed.

Times Square is over here.

Chrysler Building

Empire State Building

This is the Hudson River.

We took this picture from Hoboken, New Jersey. The view to the Empire State Building was spectacular. The lights changed to blue, white, blue this night!

DID YOU KNOW...

The Hudson River will reverse direction and flow back upstream when the ocean tide is rising. The Mahican name for the river is Muh-he-kun-ne-tuk and means "the river that flows both ways."

walking and biking path on the Brooklyn Bridge—sooooooo neat

Did you know you can walk from Brooklyn to Manhattan across the East River? The Brooklyn Bridge has a pedestrian and bike path that runs above the road level. My dad took this photo from the bridge. That's the Manhattan Bridge you see and way off in the distance is the Empire State Building.

The United Nations sits on international territory in New York City.

Empire State Building

United Nations Headquarters

One last look at Empire State Building—
pretty amazing, huh?

EMPIRE STATE

Here are some more crazy amazing FACTS I learned while in New York City ...

At the very very top of Empire State Building, there is a lightning rod, and the building actually gets struck by lightning around 23 times EVERY YEAR! Ouch man, that's got to smart!

There are something like 4,000 street-food vendors around New York City. It's a good thing I like hot dogs, kebobs, pretzels, falafels, ice cream, lemonade, I could go on foreeeeevvvveeerrrrrrr ...

Empire State Building was the first building to have 100 floors, like in the whole world. Actually, the building totally has 102 floors, but who's counting ... oh wait, I am! LOL!!!

The Empire State Building actually has its own zip code! Imagine that! I heard that the only place that has more offices in the U.S. is the Pentagon! Holy cow, that's BIG!

Did you know that the New York Subway runs all day? That's soooo like 24 hours a day! You can go anywhere at anytime. Most of it's underground and my dad said that the first underground section was opened in 1904. I guess he read that somewhere, because he's old but not THAT OLD!!

After a fast cab ride to the airport, we boarded our plane and headed home. I couldn't help but think about all the great places we saw and the cool stuff we did together. The Empire State Building is so super cool and New York City totally ROCKS!

My dad says I'm the best assistant he has ever had. I'm major excited to see where our next trip will take us!

See Ya!
Mackenzie

Our cabbie was a super fast driver. We made it to the airport in lightning speed!